THE MONTHS

Susan Wicks has published seven collections of poetry, four of them with Bloodaxe Books: *The Months* (2016), *House of Tongues* (2011), *De-iced* (2007) and *Night Toad: New & Selected Poems* (2003), which included a selection from three earlier books published by Faber: *Singing Underwater*, winner of the Aldeburgh Poetry Festival Prize; *Open Diagnosis*, which was one of the Poetry Society's New Generation Poets titles; and *The Clever Daughter*, a Poetry Book Society Choice which was shortlisted for both T.S. Eliot and Forward Poetry Prizes. *The Months*, *House of Tongues*, *Night Toad* and *Singing Underwater* are all Poetry Book Society Recommendations. *Lace*, a pamphlet collaboration with visual artist Elizabeth Clayman was published by Stonewood Press in 2015.

She has also published three novels, *The Key* (Faber, 1997), *Little Thing* (Faber, 1998) and *A Place to Stop* (Salt, 2012), a short memoir, *Driving My Father* (Faber, 1995), and a collection of short fiction, *Roll Up for the Arabian Derby* (Bluechrome, 2008). Her two book-length translations of the French poet Valérie Rouzeau, *Cold Spring in Winter* (Arc, 2009) and *Talking Vrouz* (Arc, 2013) have between them won the Scott Moncrieff Prize for Translation from French and the Oxford-Weidenfeld Prize for Literary Translation, and been shortlisted for the International Griffin Prize for Poetry and the Poetry Society's Popescu European Poetry Translation Prize.

SUSAN WICKS

The Months

BLOODAXE BOOKS

ISBN: 978 1 78037 290 7

First published 2016 by
Bloodaxe Books Ltd,
Eastburn,
South Park,
Hexham,
Northumberland NE46 1BS.

www.bloodaxebooks.com
For further information about Bloodaxe titles
please visit our website or write to
the above address for a catalogue.

Supported using public funding by
**ARTS COUNCIL
ENGLAND**

Cover design: Neil Astley & Pamela Robertson-Pearce.

Printed in Great Britain by Bell & Bain Limited, Glasgow, Scotland, on
acid-free paper sourced from mills with FSC chain of custody certification.

for Emily and Pat

ACKNOWLEDGEMENTS

Acknowledgements are due to the editors of the following publications in which some of these poems have already appeared, sometimes under different titles: *Ambit, Cyphers, Magma, The North, Poetry Ireland Review, Poetry London, The Poetry Review, The Rialto, The Times Literary Supplement,* and *Hands and Wings: Poems for Freedom from Torture* (ed. Dorothy Yamamoto, White Rat Press, 2015).

'Tide' was commissioned by the Larkin 25 Festival and a handwritten copy is archived at the University of Hull.

'Southwards': from *The Truce* by Primo Levi, translated by Dr Stuart Woolf, published by The Bodley Head and reproduced by permission of The Random House Group Ltd.

I am particularly grateful for residencies at the MacDowell Colony and Hedgebrook, as well as Brisons Veor, on Cape Cornwall, which gave me time and space to work on poems in the collection.

Section 4 of 'The Months' owes a small but appreciable debt to Neil Rollinson and the French poet Michèle Métail.

Special thanks too to my poet friends and particularly to the first readers of this collection in manuscript, Moniza Alvi, Mara Bergman, Robin Chapman and Caroline Price and to Edna Zapanta-Manlapaz, who made me think again.

CONTENTS

Childhood

I am the attic and the island,
fir tree brushing the window, shipwreck,
whalebones at the tideline washed clean.

I am a mattress of fresh straw,
a hide of interwoven branches
where the stars come in.

I am the hand-turned bowl
with a grain like satin,
filled to the brim with warm froth.

I am cheese and no cheese.
In my salt-stained tatters, hairy as a monkey
gibbering from a deep cave

I call myself Ben Gunn. Or Peter, goat-boy;
Clara at the cliff-edge while her wheelchair
buckets down into the ravine.

Each evening when the mountains turn to flame
I am talking parrot, I am, I am
sixty men on a dead prosthetic limb.

I am buried treasure, undiscovered, homesick
exile in a polished room,
my cache of rolls inedible as bricks.

Somewhere a blind grandmother
lights her driftwood beacon on the beach
ever less often, no longer hoping for my return.

April is the month for cutting up a map with scissors

You cut along the roads, this palimpsest
of tangled lines, your blades excising
country lanes, a thin blue length of river.

Or contour-lines: a landscape's close-whorled web
could lose its top, become a thumb-shaped hole and never
find itself again. And you will never

find your way back down. You let the scissors wander,
shaving the railway from its shaded bank,
the tracks from their flood plain, a bridge from what flows under,

blocks or pips of churches from their cross.
You join the dotted footprints of a path
with one clean slit, so the path itself's erased, and all that's left

is a line between two fields, and you can never
go that way again. You sever wood
from orchard, orchard from reed-clumped marsh; manoeuvre

deftly in and out along the fretted coast,
trimming land from water – high tide now or low?
You'll never know. The map

falls from your fingers in green shreds, a new high water
drowns the coastal strip, begins to lap
the land and grass is pushing up

through paper, flocks of exotic scraps alight and flutter
round your feet, jade-green as sea or parkland, curling,
blown off-course, like feathers.

Bike-path

It could take the best part of your life
to find a path like this
protected from the public thoroughfare by rocks,
meandering along between old trees
beside a river, skirting warehouses,
over a plank bridge.

Sometimes you almost gave up
and stopped to read the map,
tracing your route from fold
to fraying fold – not these wheel-trap surfaces
broken and scored by ice
as if some beast had dragged its claws across.

But now you keep on going till it joins a street
of condos, little kids on bikes,
and suddenly it's hard to keep your face straight
as this small boy explains
the signage of the three-way intersection
and what it means.

This is the scenic way: all sense of where you were
is lost. Though in fact it's not that far
from anywhere. And look,
you got to see those birds,
these greening leaves, this butterfly that flutters up
like blackened paper to your handlebars.

Where

Where do geese go when they fly north
too soon? This morning in the lane
they straggled overhead, a wishbone skein
of ten or fifteen. Already from the south
I heard them weeks ago
creaking above me through the air at dusk –
and then the cold. Eighteen below,
each pond a cataract of ice. Where did they go?

You laughed. The birds weren't stupid,
surely they'd just turn round
and head back south, searching for softer ground
where the grasses weren't starved white,
where shoots poke through the moss, and insects
rise in sunlight – flutter down

to open water. I wouldn't wish anything dead.
But I like to think of them
not turning – stretching their stubborn necks
to splinter a runnel in soft ice
as it meets around their bodies, feathers
frosted hard as spines, and under the skin
a seam of fat all but worked out,
their webbed feet churning the deep black.

Runner

You'd hardly call it running, yet he runs
low to the ground, a sort of fluent
hobble, in the shallow valley of the gutter,
trusting the cars and buses
to see him and steer round him, while his feet
push gently against the tarmac over and over
and the earth shoves back, as if
to say I'm here, still running, look, and you will never
beat me, bone and ligaments and cartilage
at ankle hip and knee
crunching to hard hot lumps, and in his legs an ache
pulsing like veins from heels to lower back –
as if he knows all that
and more. As if he's run for miles already,
days or weeks or years, in every kind of weather,
unfazed by the downs and ups,
the roads and red-brick paths, the way the rain
has soaked his singlet to a new transparent skin,
the way the winter sun
closes his weeping eyes, or frost
surrounds him with a cloud of breath,
the way he looks
for turning bikes and dawdling kids with bags
and knuckled roots, how after a few weeks
he hardly feels
his body, those familiar knots
of flesh and blood, but only the cold scatter
from his water-bottle as he raises it
and glugs, the way it falls back lighter.

Listen

Will you come into the lounge, Dorothy?
Will you sit out in your chair?
But you'd rather listen to the radio,
the voice that is always there.

Will you let us lift you, Dorothy? Won't you rise
like a prophet into thin air
or sand or gold to be deposited
in the Bank of England? You're not sure.

Will you have tea, my love? Oh, won't you please
sit with the others? But they're all old
and you've no time for old. You shut your eyes
and hear your husband's voice – its thread

of reason in the maze
you wander in together to the sun-dial dead
at the centre. In your ear
he whispers *Darling*, as he takes you there.

Boston Fair

Walking the Haven path to town I saw it all again,
  her sideways mouth, that escaping blob of lip,
    her cheeks sucked hollow by each breath –
      and heard the voiceless whisper of her voice
        that croaked, 'You're special,' and 'It'll be all right.'

The path was slick along the dike,
  the boats and barges risen almost level with the quay.
  A flood of living bodies spewed us into the place
    where a carousel of horses turned unridden,
      two black flourishes like speech-marks on each nose

for nostrils, so the nostrils seemed to float
  rising and falling on a sea of gilt –
    except for one small girl who, huddled to her mount,
      came round and round unchanged. We turned
        to leave, and glimpsed another ride

lit up in pink and mauve – its skeleton façade
  and line of waiting couples tightly interlaced.
  And as we walked away the moon began to rise
    over flat fields, the shouts and music fading
      at our backs. The Stump visible for miles.

Kite-Surfers, Useless Bay

(for Meg Day)

One night I dreamed there was a child
inside me, turning a liquid cartwheel of delight –
and woke to see surfers' kites
over Useless Bay, two upside-down smiles
swooping out and back, two stick-men riding the tide,
criss-crossing. The kites had no need of them.
They were their own thing
flying, dancing their own dance.

I thought of how we met,
your smile that reminds me of my daughter's –
how I'd like to lift you on wide wings like that
bald eagle's as it lifted from its perch
above the littered driftwood of the beach
so you could hover
watching the surfers' kites
scratch their disappearing wakes on water.

One night I dreamed my name was Bald
and when I felt my crown
the hair there was soft and thin
as a baby's. Tonight the kites are furled
somewhere inland. You curl on the window-seat
like a schoolgirl, smile
your downturned smile and shrug and tell us how
it is, before the chemo starts again.

Eperlèques

This wood we walk in has been landscaped
by bombs – this pond on the north side
where we watch the fish home in
on a piece of crumbled bread and shine
red-gold through water like a rayed sun –
was all man-made, the basin hollowed out
by a tallboy in 1943. A mini-quake,
and a slab of concrete toppled from the brow
of the bunker, though its grey face
has hardly wrinkled. And here outside
on platforms are the implements it takes
to wage a war – the guns and jeeps
and cattle-trucks, the military bikes,
a V1 mounted on a ramp, ready to explode
into the trees. Inside, the floor's been raised
a foot or two so visitors can still
walk down into the dark. In a lit niche
a V2 stands like a statue, while a card
lays bare its mysteries – its fragile neck
and sloping shoulders, hint of waist
and hips, and, deep inside, a hidden chamber
where the mix ignites. The armoured point,
the weight, the height, the documented crater,
everything is here. We look and learn,
walking from one station to the next,
pressing the buttons to hear messages
in fluent French or English, German, Dutch –
a *son et lumière* without the light.
The actors, male and female, do their bit
between the reminiscences of slaves,
the grieving music at each mention of a death.
A din of bangs and whistles re-enacts
bombardment – then an uplifting snatch
of Beethoven's Choral: it all bleeds
together, a quartet of languages
with our own voices and the songs of birds
flitting bright-eyed between the leaves.

Second Goodbye

She wasn't expecting to see anyone
but herself in the train window, their goodbyes
a hand-to-mouth, on-tiptoe blur
of fingers glimpsed through swimming eyes,
her head at the lowered window –
but suddenly there he is,
this madman, banking, diving like a swallow
as if to scratch his flight across glass.

Somehow that lifting thing
can't be what it seems,
the glitter on its wings
and what she knows of war can't be the same –
though tonight he will be over some dark coast
and she's a tiny figure on a snaking train.

Southwards

(after Primo Levi, The Truce*)*

The train ran through endless fields,
dark towns and villages
and forests which I thought had disappeared
from the heart of Europe. In the dark
a village slept, an unlit town. Deep in the heart
of forests, conifers and birches
struggled upwards, fighting for the sun.

The forests were dense and wild
and have not disappeared
from the heart of Europe. Out there in the dark
between the sleeping towns
the conifers and birches still compete
for sunlight. Slowly a train
forces its way forward as if in a tunnel.

Deep under the heart
of Europe even now
a locomotive snorts its head of steam
to a roof of intertwining branches; rumbles on
towards Rzeszóv, Przemysl with its grim
fortifications, Lemberg the skeleton city
where we got down.

Poinsettia

You open your tight red bracts
palm upwards to all-comers in the hall,
hardly seeming to feel
the draught in the open doorway.
Shouldn't your silhouette be skeletal?

Easter has come and gone,
the baby grown
all ribs and loin-cloth, crucified,
and yet the flower in you persists,
still unconvinced

that hope is yellow now, and winged,
and every crimson thing is stripped
and laid in boxes on a nest
of paper in the loft
with tinsel, lights in tangled strings.

Shouldn't you be withered now, give way
to crocuses and tulips, younger flames?
Or else turn back the clock
or forwards, till the time
of dark and birth and candles comes again.

Shoes

(Lisa Milroy, oil on canvas 176.5 x 226 cm)

They must be a kind of code –
a trio of four-letter words.
Life, they say, a woman's, neat
and highly polished, narrow feet,
a touch of whim, fatigue. Or *Love*
(constricted, but still keeping up
appearances, and failing
though they rarely disagree). Or *Hate*
she can see her face in –
pointed toes aligned
and heels that could spike his chest.
Or simply *Fuck*, eyes teasing,
shoes thrown off, and yes,
perhaps she's offering herself
as feet, as twelve immaculate black pairs
that open to the heat
like mussels and we glimpse the gold.
Her twenty-four clean soles
delicately tap tap
their playful *Mayday, Mayday*,
while we ask, *Is it too late?*

Not Waving

Rattling through suburbs towards London
I see it each time – there, over to the left
on a flat roof, a disused bathtub
like the one my father-in-law kept
in his own back garden just before he died,
collecting raindrops. Not so easy
to get rid of when you're old and disconsolate

and won't be helped. But this
is full of legs – sometimes a bare toe
just poking over, sometimes an amputated thigh –
the limbs of a jiggling, jostling crowd
of hard-fleshed women, moulded in bisque
or wood-pulp, plastic or flaking plaster –
you'd need to reach and touch them to say which.

What can they be doing, face down
in dark? I seem to hear them gasp
and flounder in their puddle of green slime,
banging their hollow torsos one against another
in a clash of holes. A flaking finger
enters a shoulder socket, meets
nothing but perished rubber, and withdraws.

Could they be real women, dead
and bloodlessly dismembered, pulled
from a park somewhere? They're only dolls,
shop-window dummies with no clothes
but the rain and fog, veils of volcanic dust,
the orange haze of streetlamps –
a poor man's strip-tease.

Or are these the legs of angels?
Ought we to pray
as we rush towards Waterloo? They shine
under drizzle, they defeat us when we try

to join the dots. And who are we?
They're naked, pink, not waving, not in pain
like us, and seemingly permanent.

A Room Called 'Lifeboat'

My lifeboat's sea-blue-spotted with an aqua throw,
pillows patterned with roses. A rope of shells
hangs lifeless from a rail. A model ship with metal sails
is for shipwrecked souls to play with. Every night alone
I gulp salt breaths; each morning, surfacing,
I shake out my teal and turquoise towels of distress.

A wreath of hessian and raffia suggests
what flowers were, which insects flew on land,
what land once was. A giant oyster on the window-sill
reveals that life has left – yet something dead
can decorate a room, the blues and corals of its deep insides
clean-scoured. A mirror perfectly positioned on the wall

can catch the sun. And maybe this ceramic jar's enough
to stop a floor capsizing? Over these roofs the same
crows and gulls and pigeons cry or laugh,
flitting from ridge to ridge, the weather rough or calm.

26

Man and Dog, Cromer

Two men with dogs are striding across the sand
in perfect sync, two padded torsos square themselves
to mount the shingle, four pale arms keep time.
But the two dogs linger, touching noses, standing

tail to tail. They like it here
in this new-silvered mirror, where a different air
riffles their fur. They stop and sniff at shells
or worm-casts, seaweed, other noses stopping to sniff theirs.

It's late already; running, their light legs
hardly dent the water, while the men march on
to higher ground, a bulldozed ramp of dry, and whistle –
and the dogs must follow, one of their masters gone.

On Cromer Cliffs

It was an odd, botched, home-made thing
of polystyrene, a pair of wings
covered with coloured paper – blue and red,
a flash of white – the union flag
but half-erased. There, above the sands,
no body, cockpit, fuselage – only a flat V
where the two blades met across
a small black box awaiting his command.

It's stress-relief. He laughed.
Escaping from the wife. He held it up
between his thumb and first two fingers like a boy
throwing a paper dart
and lumbered to the cliff-edge,
let it swoop
towards the tideline – but his hands were there
grasping already, clenched on the remote
and opening the throttle, shouting
Go and *Climb, you fucker* till it looped the loop.

Those climbs and barrel-rolls
still buzz inside my head – the way he stood
right at the edge to throw it, while his heart
beat faster, pumping like a pilot's
on a first solo flight – how for half a breath
he must have left himself
to fall between the shells and seaweed on the beach
with no one's saving hand at the controls.

The World Tells Me Otherwise

Yesterday on that lip of sunlit cliff
the grass was full of purple crocuses – more like the silk
of tattered vestments than a bruise, the sea itself
a calm grey-green, closing and unclosing its skin
like an eyelid. Down there on the sand
dogs capered, people walked or jogged or picked up stones
and skimmed them, couples held hands.
And old men marvelled how the wall had been rebuilt
twice in as many winters, and was new again
and better than it was, and painted cream.

House with White Shutters

It was small, but ours – two up,
two halfway up, two down
and every forward-facing window
fringed with cosmetic shutters
that changed the look of the façade
the way two painted eyes
with pencilled eyebrows make a face
too wide awake
too soon. Those tight-packed, lived-in storeys –
master bedroom in flocked gold,
magenta hallway, yellow and green downstairs
with a wall of brittle cork
(though the muffled barks
and curses still came through). Outside,
a pocket garden full of roses,
a lawn I could cut with scissors,
an ersatz wishing-well
full of purple iris where we'd gather snails
to set them free. Yet we were
happy, weren't we? Those nights I cried
picking up puzzle pieces,
and the day I knocked the hi-fi on its shelf
with the tube of the vacuum-cleaner
so ever after
the Maiden tripped on and on
in her groove of dying and I seemed to see
myself, my eyes squeezed shut, my back
to the storage heater, chin on my knees. Then that other
day of silent snowfall when I dragged the girls
behind me up the slippery hill to school.

The night we stared
all four of us together at a window
high at the back, while a house on the horizon
spluttered gouts of fire
and burned on sleepless
to the song of sirens into early morning.

O

(for Rachel Cusk)

I wore it in my sleep. In waking hours
it clinked on tables, on the steering-wheels of cars,
jiggled on keyboards, gleamed in photographs,
passed through detector gates without a peep

and came wherever I did. Forty years
and suddenly they show: a welt of reddened skin
circles my finger, burns for what might have been
until I died. Something wants emptiness.

I slip it off, and still my finger flakes
and itches, blisters, wears this scarlet ghost
of gold. I'm wedded to an O my hand dislikes

– while I go ringless, where my daughters' names
are not-yet-thought-of, where my mother's ring
slipped from its dead finger through the flames.

Lebkuchen-haus

(for Emily and Rebecca)

She stands hunched over her stick
in the doorway, her white eyes
searching between the trees
for what? Whoever comes
is young and guileless, brittle
as matchsticks, new face painted on.

Behind her, her ginger house
is full of dark, its steep-pitched roof
iced hard. She sees the boy and girl
approaching, guards her entry-holes –
the arch of her front door's mouth,
her ox-eye window puckered like a rose.

Nothing to keep but this stale cake,
a handful of sweets fallen from the sky
and stuck to the roof like slugs
or gobs of fungus, white-tailed rats.
Yet here are six-pointed stars
in pink or yellow, her inverted heart.

Through a dust of white she sees
tree-trunks with goblin faces.
Beyond, a drift of crumbs,
a flick of feathers; that bright pane
of woodman's hut, his pile of wood,
the children on the threshold, hand in hand.

Where has her life gone
as she weighed and measured, baked
the bricks of her own house
and set them steaming on a rack in sun –
as she waited, watching for something
fragile as bird-bones, asking to be broken?

Boeuf Miroton

Our days are shrinking now to single sentences
between two deep parentheses of dark
and so are we. The path outside
is slippery with fish-skins of black leaves.
Inside I'm making something
called *Boeuf Miroton*, the name
casting its own light – a dot, a bird, a floating hat,
a wonder. Onions melt in butter
while I measure flour, make stock,
grind breadcrumbs, pour white wine.
The yellow quinces strung along the fence
begin to glow, lighting this late-afternoon November.
Yes, okay, so this is where we are, our girls long gone,
their little clutching hands that caught
and almost tripped us. Now I can cross a room like God
to music, to the yellow light
of rotting fruit, mouthing a foreign word.

Winter Saffron

Almost too late, and the dew already falling,
I can feel it, as I reach to fumble
the line towards me, bundle the clothes in half
into the basket, breathing their smell of clean.
The sheets lean in against me,
wrap me like colder skin.
Knickers flap their bleached bunting.

This late September evening,
I can almost touch it, something is changing –
a blade of starlings whirrs
through dusk. A fairy ring in grass
lies broken. Somewhere a clock
shivers into life, the daylight draining
to a distant yellow rectangle of kitchen

where my younger daughter
sings as she cooks. She angles the board and scrapes it
into a waiting pan, her face is pink through steam,
her lips are synching
some old sixties song – Tom Lehrer, is it? – and I'm looking in

at my own life, its shrinking winter spaces,
pots and pans – while I clutch the basket
to my hip and stagger
up the path in darkness where a breath of mint and wine
and saffron meets me and I see
I've left the kitchen door half-open.

THE MONTHS

(for Emily)

'Most women dream more when they are pregnant. The reason
for this is not known.'

GORDON BOURNE, FRCS, FRCOG, *Pregnancy* (1972)

'So frail, that bus! I kept expecting it to fall over and burn.'

RUSSELL HOBAN, *Amaryllis Night and Day*

1 *December 2012*

That month everything seemed to break.
When you came, we did that walk,
the three of us, an uphill trek
through woods and rotting leaves, to overlook
the furrowed fields, the saturated ground
of late November, day already dark
before what should be nightfall. Everything broke –
my watch, its 'lifetime' battery gone flat,
the bathroom time-switch, liquid-crystal screen
expressionless.
                    Our hands no longer moved,
our time stood still; the halo of blue light
each morning on our bedroom wall went out,
while something sent my inbox half-berserk,
receiving new-old emails black on black.
Then yet another walk, this time with Pat
between two treatments, when the floods shrank back
to leave the meadows smooth, inscrutable with mud,
the fences strung with draggled ropes of grass,
till darkness caught us and we floundered ankle-deep
and laughed – because what could we do
but laugh?
                    And then, in spite of everything
you broke your news – at Christmas. As I lay
one evening drifting, radio on low, and sick
of broken things, the angel's face
came up all smeared with river-silt and weed,
his wing-tips dripping mud – and said
All hail! He called you his *most highly favoured lady*,
bowed his reckless head. And you responded, *Gloria!*
and someone in the future sang it back.

36

February 1978

I echoed, *Gloria!*,
remembering that night
in Dublin, taxi lights reflected in the wet
where I stood shivering, those blood-clots
big as a small fist – my first child lost
in Holles Street, the tears
that seemed to come from nowhere as I sat
at Belfield on the top deck of a bus
– then barely three months later,
back in England, a distaste
for coffee, my mid-morning cigarette
impossible, a roiling in my gut...
And I rejoiced
to think of that house-hunting, jobbing life
of language classes – marking scripts
and almost throwing up
with John in shock
at what it meant to teach,
while I played Scrabble nightly
with my mum, made bread.
Sometimes the sunlit fields were sharp
with frost, and snow
fell horizontal. In my sleep
my parents died of nose-bleed, yet
one lunchtime as my mother did the washing-up
we heard a shout
and when we ran to help no help
was needed – only the window's glass
awash with red.
We ran outside and saw
the basket overhead, we heard
the gas-jet, waved; we watched it start to rise
and clear the next-door trees
and slowly pass,
peeling its blood-shadow from the grass.

2 *January 2013*

'You'd better both sit down,' you said
before you told us, over stale mince-pies
with mascarpone: this new life
might or might not have a father
or a place to live – just a two-room flat
above an antique-shop. And yet. Onscreen
another Clara dances with her *casse-noisette*
clutched to her breast, and suddenly the tree's
enormous. Covent Garden Live: between the acts
we see the watchers putting on their jackets,
shuffling from their seats. You're telling us your news
and then you're gone, and working, living where you live
alone, and we are toasting you in Crémant de Bourgogne
brought back last August, hoarded understairs
in the wine-rack's honeycomb.

Upstairs, I strip the tree and pack away
the tinsel, baubles, lights. We raise
the sash and lower the remains
from the open window on a length of rope
like a black fishbone into the waves of cold
as cats come nosing, curious. A few more days,
and John is leaning into the optician's bowl
of lights, to greet each pin-prick flash
with finger on the buzzer – though this time
it seems one eye has lost the map. We're cut adrift
in a swirl of trash. Our orbit's speeding up
and only a few stars are left
to glitter and be caught, another, then another...
yet in the farthest corner of our sky's
a small new planet no one yet has named.

Coleslaw. A need for something fresh.
The coiled white intricacy of a cabbage-head
sliced thinner, thinner. *Cabbages are cheap*
and nourishing, and good, we said,
misquoting Strindberg. Carrot-shavings,
onion, mayonnaise. I gobbled dish on dish
to ward off sickness, while my parents talked in bed
in tones of elderly defeat,
I couldn't bear it. *Let me find a flat,*
a caravan, a cowshed – anywhere
to have my baby in! And yet
crocuses stuck yellow fingers through the grass
at Sparrow's Green, and on TV
the shadow-women danced
for *Bond, James Bond*, across the barrel of a gun.
And every Tuesday night my dad drove John and me
out to the Best Beech for a game of darts.
I watched and waited, fingering a flight
of watered blue. And on days off we tried
to find somewhere to live – a seller's market,
everything snapped up as soon as it appeared,
until the day my mother pointed to that ad
in the *Courier – 86, Queen's Road* – my dad already
reaching for his keys. Hands cupped
against the glass, we stoop together, try to see inside:
a basement dining-room in green
and mustard, a magenta hall,
a papered rectangle of kitchen wall
with blooms as big as saucers. Nothing to be done
but wait – one hour, two hours,
until whoever placed the ad returns,
and makes a cup of tea, and we can all
shake hands. And then
outside it's dark again, I'm in my mother's kitchen
retching, cutting a cabbage to fine shreds
for coleslaw, back to the Best Beech –
and John this time the winner,
whooping when he makes the double top.

3 *February 2013*

Eleven weeks. Your baby's growing, big
as my little finger. On the phone last night,
I don't know how, I let your secret out
like a cartoon cat and down the snowy street
it scampered, punching wheelie-bins
till it knocked itself out flat
on a lamp-post, and came bouncing back –
boi-oi-oing! – like a punch-bag on a stick.

Now our new instructor shouts
the moves of boxercise. A shadow-cloud
of central-heating gases floats across
the gym's white face. This morning I looked out
and down through falling snow and saw
a bee half-buried on the bedroom window-sill
like a blackened finger, caught
and frozen vertical, up to its tiny waist.

Che gelida... Snow lies inches deep
in drifts and hollows, slowly melts
into dry air. I'm reading *A Life's Work*
a second time, remembering
the way a mother's future is usurped.
But Phil's been offered a new job
near where you live. One morning you and I
set out in icy darkness for the hospital

and as we're crawling down that hill
through Nutfield, all our roof's packed snow
slides down to cataract our windscreen white.
You stop. And I leap out and rake away
the cold so we can see. That day
we see a half-transparent baby like a fish
in dark – a head, and what might be a fist,
and something pulsing unmistakably – a heart.

April 1978

That was the month with the blank page.
Even now my hand shakes
as I turn it; at the unbroken white
I catch my breath, remembering.
Yet now, my mum cremated twenty years,
no words I could hope to write
can bring it back.

Morning. Too soon for breakfast,
too early yet for sun.
My mother, me. Both of us half-asleep,
unguarded – and then both of us
half-mute with fury. What was our row about?
Nothing I wanted to record.
Even then I was incredulous.

Nothing. Or something infinite-
ly trivial that would make me laugh
if I had written it, and her as well
if she were here. Later, we visited my aunt,
her cactus one great flower-burst of red.
The secret is to stop it having babies,
was that what she said?

What's left has been made safe:
the letting-out of trousers; *Star Wars* on TV;
a plate of chicken biriani on my own
at the Taj Mahal – and dreams
of you as a red-haired boy-child, born
like a silk scarf out of a top hat
to greet us grinning, already articulate.

Your baby's fully formed
and growing – and might have a home.
You've seen a cottage – two rooms down,
three up, a shower under the eaves
where a six-foot man won't fit,
the garden shaded by a giant eucalyptus – yet
it's somewhere. Meanwhile I'm in York
(though half with you in Dorking) while my brain
riffles through poem-snapshots of Berlin
I've promised to translate.
(At Anhalter Bahnhof an abandoned terminus
still waits beneath a whitish crust
of pigeon-droppings; in Viktoriapark
a man-made waterfall runs down
unstoppable; while, facing east,
Der Rufer cups his hands to his bronze mouth
and shouts his silent shout
across a ghost of wall and nobody can tell
if what he cries is peace
or SOS.) Up here we shiver in a medieval room
with a bag of limes and lemons,
curl our icy fingers to a warm cup
and think of Neruda. *Can you write about
the things they smell of?*
But they smell of nothing,
each fruit hard, sealed taut
on its own juice
till we cut them open
and the aromatic oil spurts up.

May 1978

Remember that bit in *Blow-up*, when
he magnifies a tiny section of the shot
of someone's lifeless body sticking out
and we strain to focus? It was a bit like that
but tactile. Not a quickening
exactly – more a losing speed
till our whole life seemed to be slowing down,
thinned to a single heartbeat, and we touched –
you rippling like a fish
through veils of seaweed, me the tank of flesh
that felt you move. The faintest flick
then stillness. Then another, amplified
as you swam closer. In that slow-mo world
where vendors temporised and life seemed half-asleep
and manuscripts might still be taken, where in dreams
I schussed downhill on skis – one rallentando night
when John had cooked risotto and my father sliced
each rice-grain into quarters with his knife –
I couldn't bear it. Out
we fell to crawl the village pubs till closing-time
and stumble back down lanes
through mist and dark, half-cut,
invincible – Achilles or the flying arrow homing in –
as you kicked the wall between us
thinner, thinner, beating the distances
to halves and quarters then in half again.

Is it a he or she? At the next scan
you'll close your eyes: this child's
a child, itself, not offered up
to our imaginings. Down here
above the Tamar's banks of tidal mud
the Calstock viaduct
opens its airy mouth-parts to the sky
and swallows grass
and leaning masts and rushes,
gulps the tide
and lets it trickle out...
We visit Pat again and find her thinner,
too much in pain this time to laugh
and yet she does. And afterwards
at Lydford Gorge through winter trees
and softly falling snow
we photograph the water's sheer
white ribbon barely wavering,
then track the stream uphill
as it bucks and plunges,
arches its sleek neck,
to the Witch's Cauldron – and admire
the smoothness of those sides
scoured clean by water
reeling clockwise,
that dark belly-pot of rock
where nothing can stay alive.

A man in a white coat
raises his syringe and squeezes,
squeezes, waits for a few clear drops
to fall and turns – and deep inside
you scream. I shriek and scratch and bite
until they let you live –
and I wake up. Inside I feel you move.
And we are moving, out
at last to 86 Queen's Road – new bed,
new fold-out sofa hefted from the street
and up the steps, my mother
hoovering, while on the stairs
my dad grubs carpet-tacks with an old knife.
The dining-table travels up in state
from Horsham: *Just you wait*
till the top's refinished, you won't recognise
it then! – but thirty-five years on
it's as it was: the story of a life –
though whose is not yet clear.
My relatives are everywhere,
noticing what cries out to be done
and quietly doing it, and leaving. Late that night
we lie in bed awake
in a smell of new-bought mattress, hear
the clock strike one and two
and four. We're finally alone.
The house ticks under a new weight
of furniture. Our bodies ache.

Our window-cleaner must have lain
in bed all day for months, or died – each pane

of every single window's silted half-opaque
with dried-on drops. For all our sakes

I try to reach each corner, get it clear,
at least inside. And it *was* clear

the day you two moved out, our men
lumping your futon downstairs to the van

while upstairs in a pool of sun
I packed your pots and pans. But then,

alone with Phil on that last run, the two of us
downhill through woods, your exodus

complete, oh why did I open my big mouth
and say how are you, why did I let his breath

mist up my windows? Late that night
I dreamed that somewhere beyond fright

a voice instructed me to clear a school
of staff and students, and I did. Then like a fool

I lingered in the classroom half-awake
as on the walls electric heaters rose like snakes

in my direction, sizzled, and I understood
my time was up. No blood,

no pain, no chance to wonder what it meant
for life to leave, or where it went –

but only, *This is it then, this is how it ends.*

July 1978

That month for me was loud. No scan
back then, or not for us: I meet my new GP.
He lets me hear your heart, and what I hear's
an army coming nearer – a whole regiment
on horseback, pounding the parched ground
in a storm of dust. By then at school
the girls are more or less beyond control,
crazy with giggles. On the Wadhurst train
I hear them and feel lucky: we're delayed
the day the teachers get their dressing-down,
and then again on Speech Day, when,
apparently, a half-cut colleague stands to cheer
each student's small achievement or success.
That's the week John's dad decides to come,
a fortified green bottle in each hand –
the day our shabby furniture's pushed back
and carpet-men are at it with their hammers –
while my parents, not to be outdone,
wheel in a thing unearthed among a friend's
unwanted junk – an ancient, bulbous Frigidaire
from a 1950s movie. Someone plugs it in.
We wait for it to hiss and clunk and stutter.
Nothing happens. Is it just *too* old? And yet
it seems to hear us. Look! Its rubber lips are sealed
on milk in frosted bottles, butter
hardening to bricks. An icy vapour
greets us in silence when we kneel.

Something is happening to time,
stretching and compressing like a worm
or severed by a blade. Where have they gone,
those crabshells packed with light
and darker meat, when I had lunch with friends
in Cromer? Where's the night
when John and I
got up at 2 a.m.
and drove to Gatwick,
through a sleeping town
deserted but for one young man
weaving along the pavement towards home?

And what's happened to Greece in all this –
our summer holiday months early –
all that sudden rain
that spilled from gutters
after the swallows' acrobatic flight
across the harbour?
Where are the tamarisks and oleanders,
that dried-up snake-skin curling like a finger
inches from my front wheel on the verge?
And meanwhile you and Phil have gone to Brittany to doze
in deckchairs while the barbecue still sizzles, hours
gone awol. So it's no surprise

your sister's asked us for a clock
as wedding-gift. But Pat is out of pain
and soon the summer proper will begin –
the little train at Thassos snake along the dock
beside the restaurants,
uphill between the pines,
each open truck
lit up and full of children. Under the pale green
of a cotton duvet-cover on the back of Bridget's bedroom door
dangles her wedding-dress –
life-size and almost human,
full of breath.

August 1978

Yes, that was it, the month when time
at last began to tell. The friends who came
and stayed to joke and drink, and no one cared
if I caught or missed the bus
to my ante-natal class. I missed it, took another one instead
in tears to my parents' house, and rode with them
through miles of dappled lanes
to a barn of Moses baskets, playpens, cots and pushchairs – and
    returned
the owner of a reconditioned Marmet pram
to see *Twelfth Night*, the RSC, in Southborough, and dream
of poor Malvolio (his *keep me in darkness, and do all they can
to face me out of my wits*). This time
I make it to the hospital, where they prepare us for
the *blood-clots big as tea-cups*. Then the end of term
at last, and John released, delirious.
We're off to Norfolk, to the only rented boat
that's still for rent. At walking pace
we nose up weed-grown rivers, chug our way upstream
under weeping birches, moor at Horsey Staithe
(I'm reading Iris Murdoch), push on north and east
between flat fields until
we spy what might be dunes, and enter a canal
that narrows, narrows, stops short of the sea.

By now, in late July,
you're in Northumberland, away
at Throssel Hole, to meditate:
you've lifted yourself out
among the Buddhist monks, or in.
Back in late June
you were here with us, your dress
a swelling plum, and Bridget came downstairs
a bride. Under the trailing white
wisteria I hear her still repeat
her vows through falling petals. Then too soon
the bride and groom are gone
and I am gently freeing my bouquet
from its ribbon binding, taking out the dead
to Wimbledon's white noise
pock pock look right
look left pock pock. Each night
I burn or over-salt the food, re-read
that Lawrence biog passed on by my friend who died –
how he and Frieda ranted at each other, fought
in Zennor, Florence, Mexico
and Taos, while he wrote and wrote.

One afternoon we drive
to yours to meet Phil's father and his wife
at a pub in Friday Street. Before we leave
I climb the narrow stairs of your small house
and see the baby's things already stacked –
a cot, a pile of babygros
in shades of green and yellow, white
and beige. And that same week
we walk to Trinity to see the *Figaro* on screen
from Glyndebourne. All the lit way back
we laugh, we want to sing: alive in my mind's eye
a Cherubino, piquant and delicious,
neither girl nor boy.

September 1978

Our Norfolk Odyssey is over.
Now in dreams our house is built on sand
or slimy rock. In waking hours

I try to shore it up – choose names (you're Emily
or William), bare my moony breasts
and unripe nipples to the nurse to be assessed,

visit the ward at Pembury to see them bath
a newborn baby. Watching, I become
my parents' only child again

in a line of fostered babies, every one
a slick young frog supported at the neck
by my mum's firm hand, each kick

a small surprise that saturates us both.
I wonder if the whole of the South-east
is full of grown-up babies she once washed

and if one day I meet one in the street
will he still know me, sniff me like a dog
and lick my hand? Our little house

is sliding, I am motion-sick
and no one knows me. I
don't know myself. It hurts to walk.

They've turned me to a pig. I close my eyes, go back –
East Somerton, St Mary's – to that ruined church
deep in the Norfolk woods, the reaching oak

that grew up through its centre, split it to the sky.

Time. No time. Time lost,
time stopped. Amid the cards and speeches, John retires
with a bottle of champagne
moulded in chocolate. Now he can break
his past in hollow pieces like a childhood egg.
We trade our two old cars
for something shared. And you
are also leaving work, in tears. I lose my keys,
and hunt for them all morning,
find them later in a pile of clothes
put out for Oxfam, while our car remains
a tight-sealed box.
                              One stifling day
we catch the train to Hastings, picnic on some rocks
with bladder-wrack and flies,
then take the cliffside lift. Despite the heat
we walk as far as Fairlight, clamber the disintegrating path
to overlook the distant glitter of a beach.
Then home again by train, with end-of-tether mothers,
fractious kids.
                    That night,
the storm, our curtained room lit white
and hailstones skittering on glass, a thunderclap
that shakes us both from sleep, our eyes
wide open, brains repeating *What?* –
each beating heart
within a two-mile distance of our street
for once in sync. It passes over, yet
something has changed:
                              next afternoon,
defrosting our small fridge, I hear a splintering
and find a dimpled boat of ice
floating intact.
                    And now again tonight
outside our kitchen windows, late,
this vernix moon flops out
gasping for sky between two sheets of cloud.

October 1978

By then my case was packed –
two nighties, one pair of warm socks,
some outsize sanitary pads,
a book of cryptic crosswords, and a note
of all the crucial numbers. Late one night
through glass we glimpse the moon
no thicker than the shaving from a thumbnail
when it should be almost full – we rush outside
and watch it swell again to its whole self
as our earth-shadow edges away.
I've ordered baby-clothes
and cry when they arrive.
At Pembury they've told us stage by stage
what labour is, invited us to try
the Entonox machine, but I'm wound up too tight
and pinned in place: your head
is bouncing on my nerves. *And yet.*
My aunt brings vegetables – tomatoes, beans
and apples – lays them on our table. *Am I one of these?*
Around your due-by-date,
my BP up, they send me off to bed
like a child while it's still light
and ice-cream vans are chiming in the street,
though John stays up revising lesson-plans till one
and bites my head off when I turn to him. And then
two days before they plan to intervene
I start to bleed. Next afternoon
my mother drives me in, while deep
inside me something almost-clenches. I undress.
She sits beside my bed and tells me endless
stories from her 1920s childhood
village full of kids
(and some of them apparently her father's)
– things she's never said
to me before – and when she leaves, I sleep.

Across the distances I strain
to hear you, catch the urgent ringing of our phone:
your baby's somehow turned himself feet down
and, even though it's Sunday, cries out to be born.

And he *is* born! The hospital's in motion –
visitors arriving, leaving, patients being wheeled
towards the exit, small girl skipping in electric trainers
through an arc of light. Outside,

the flash of sun on metal, car-park crammed
with lines of cars in waiting, as we slip away
across the roundabout, beneath the tracks, through town
and woodland, while somewhere behind us

he's already changing. Barely two days
and you'll be home, we'll watch you nursing him
and see his toes, his crumpled ears
are not like yours. He is

himself, a child, unknowable, like any child
born anywhere – in England, France
or Gaza, Syria, Iraq. Go back two weeks,
those little faces swaddled by a sheet,

their deep dilated pupils and unconscious mouths
trailing white tongues of froth
might have been his. Outside,
the eucalyptus reaches its scarred arms,

its strips of hanging skin, and lets them drop
to litter your small plot
with wishes. Nowhere to address
my *Please protect this child, that child, these children*

but to myself.

October 1978, September 2013

Morning at six. I wake
alone and leaking, bladder full
and won't be emptied – *Fucking Hell!*
Is this what pain is? No one cares
it seems. I crouch over my steel bowl
retching my guts out.
How did they dare to talk to us about control?

Here is the waist-high bed, the empty room.
Somehow the hours pass
with John beside me – gone – awake – asleep –
the drip-by-drip
of epidural to my spine, while day turns into night
and night to graveyard shift,
and one by one

the voices on the corridor go dumb,
the babies born,
the women wheeled away
towards the wards of cards and flowers and balloons
and only I am left,
the sobs and groans and screaming
swallowed up by time.

Till finally they call the registrar from sleep
and wheel me in, erect a screen
across my lower body, numb me in a wave
of nausea. And yet
his scalpel slides across my belly like a smile,
his fingers push and pull
and suddenly I hear you crying – here – alive.

I blink. It's gone. At last this maze
of mist and bollards we've been driving through
is clearing: we have come
to gaze and offer gifts. We whisper
hello, little one, forgive us
and his face contorts. He listens,
seeming to watch us out of narrowed eyes.

Real Time

Just at the edge of sight
a bubble bursts, a tiny eye blinks shut
and the lather readjusts
like a swarm of insects
massing, crawling on the pan's blue base.

Drying, it's an enamel map
that shrinks and moves, and compensates
for shrinkage, closing each lacy bight
to a line of dunes, peninsulas like fingerbones,
the dash-dot-dash of rocks.

Each minute's-worth of breath
is a crumbled cliff; each bubble's thinning walls
a collapsed house.
Each gradual withdrawal leaves
a halo gleaming where it was.

It is so slow
you hardly see it. Nothing seems
to change – yet in a hour
it'll all be gone. The only trick's to stay
and watch it, try and separate

something from nothing, feel your nails
emit their slow white moons,
your hair curl out and up, your memories
lengthen like shadows on the grass.
This is the one real

time of our lives – these blobs of foam
ageing and imploding without a sound
as a time flows in
where nothing happens and the smallest change
is visible, and change is everything.

After Reading Jacqmin's *Le Livre de la Neige*

Almost nothing happens: a blade of grass
grows upwards, a new leaf tears its sheath
and the split lengthens, something pushes out.
The stones change colour; a cloud-shape drifts across,
its edges melting. A gleam of sun
comes and then goes.

Nothing here to kill time
or mask it, nothing to trick the mind
from its own counting. Slowly this wooden house
warms up and shifts its weight
as the rafters creak and tick. Nothing
here but heartbeats, quiet breathing

– while a spice-road of black ants
no bigger than pinheads flows
across the slate. They hesitate
and pass, and when they meet their dead
they rear and wave their feelers, make an elaborate
diversion, find the thin trail again.

Deep in the woods
a woodpecker rattles, like the long report
of a machine-gun miles away. Again.
Another standing trunk
is pierced, another insect dies.

Double Image

Relax your eyes, and what you see is words
projected onto nothing: the image separates
and seems to float,
detached. What your ballpoint said
at the far margin of a page
imprints itself on panelled wall and glass.

Now *run* and *beams* and *spider* and *unless*
hang from the ceiling, every word a flame,
transparent at the centre –
every word a shred
of blackened wick, each name
a small destruction, each a sacred text.

For One Day Only

(The gender-designation of the pool changing-rooms reversed for repairs)

As soon as I go in
I'm lost. The lockers that were here
are over there, the showers inside-out,
and where the drinking-fountain stood,
a small urinal. They have screens

to shield them as they change
while we have none –
and fewer feet of silvered glass
to find their faces lacking in.
No dryers, or just one

so high I have to stand on tiptoe,
raise my hand and wave an SOS
to turn it on. No hooks
to hang the children's clutter from.
Their lower lockers hide a shiny emptiness

– while all our lower keys
will slip their plastic wrist-bands,
gouge their ounce of flesh. And as I leave
I turn the wrong way
and see what a man sees –

that blaze of turquoise water,
fractured sun – till I meet the eyes
of a man confused
to see me here where he should be,
and almost apologise.

In the Shower

Without curtains we
are suddenly revealed
our thighs and shoulders necks
criss-crossed by rivulets.

We've come across town
to stand here naked all ages
from still a girl at school
to almost skeleton.

Some of us have scars
like smiles where babies were
or gallstones appendices
and some of us

have pumped-up breasts
with prunes for nipples
some have bellies
buttocks pitted like the moon.

Half the shower-heads have gone
the water runs
into the gutter
swirling the rafts of lather

where dull or glossy long
or short gold matted chestnut grey
or wiry white with suds
our hair collects.

Sand

Under my window a pile of pitted sand
is tidal: dumped from a truck
in the early morning, smoothed across the ground,
it comes and goes.
The yellow barriers barely move on.
Bollards warble their hollow warning to the wind.

Each morning, grain by grain
it lays itself, smooths out the wrinkles of another life
of tides and beaches. Day by day the cobbles
slowly unfurl their fan,
picked out at evening by a passing bike
that gleams through twilight, wobbles from stone to stone.

Tide

All day I have been thinking about the tide –
each time I tapped the wheel or slowed,
accelerated out of the next bend –
whether it's low or high,

whether the rocks are exposed,
the clumps of spreading weed
just under the surface, that abandoned slick
of hair at the centre of the cove –

or whether the white tongues
are licking at the faces of the cliff
from here to Sennen, and falling slowly back;
whether the sea's begun

to cover the slipway, finger the upturned boats
with flying spray; whether the stones
are dark and gleaming, the cliffside succulents
wearing their salt coat;

whether, at high or low water,
the tide is turning, slack
as ageing skin. Part of me watches it
from the inside lane – a sudden bottleneck

and there on the opposite carriageway
a car's upended, its crumpled roof
squashed against the wheel and silvered glass
hanging in cobwebs. Surely

no one can have survived.
Or in that lethal other
pile-up near Bodmin, where the yellow signs
with a black square at their centre

send us all off how far? – ten miles? fifteen? –
trapped in a slow-moving line,
blinded between tall hedges
till we join the road again.

Yet when I catch a glimpse –
at Worthing, Portsmouth, Chideock, Penzance –
it's only blue-ish, flattish, unprepossessing,
made safe by distance.

Far out, or close up in? Stopping to eat
my lunchtime sandwich, I almost sense it move
between the rows of picnic tables
in a glittering wave

– and later at the wind-farm, high
above me, where the crazy blades
are turning out of sync, a hillside stands
and semaphores as I go by.

And then I'm here. Gently
I freewheel down between stone walls
afraid of what I'll meet. I park the car
next to the cliff. And start to empty

all my luggage out. And turn. And see the tide
is as it always would be, halfway in
or out and racing, water white
with foam, the weed

submerged, a trail of salty drops
across my window glass. Can it be rain
or spray? The beach is slick,
rust-dark. The water laps

and creeps, and laps again
in all the usual places, and explodes
and falls slow-motion back, reveals
a crab, a strand of kelp, a buckled tin.

Scooping the Sea and Looking at the Horizon
(Tai Chi form; March 2011)

She lunges and leans out, extends her arm
as if to calm the waters – *There*,
she pushes them away, *and there*,
her hands say, *Go*
in quietness. The character she draws
has travelled like a wave
inhabiting one body then the next
to gather and break, spend itself in hers.

With the clean edge of her palm
she cuts what can't be seen,
seeming to smooth apart
what's barely plural. In her body's trance
the movement flows, continuous
and formal, as she balances
first on one foot, then the other,
scooping imagined water, setting it free.

She is outside herself, dispersed
among surrounding leaves,
between the overhanging green of branches
and the dappled green of grass.
She is white crane
and flying dove, a rower in mid-lake,
a woman's body taking shape as verb.

Her measured moves
remember violence and tame it
as she looks beyond this ivy-covered fence
to the horizon, seeing histories convulse –
a tide of bodies rolled in weed and silt,
towers cracking in their veils of steam
and buckled concrete – she looks out
and bends and scoops
and lets the water trickle from her cupped palm.

This Art

(Museum of Inuit Art, Toronto)

This art tells stories of a few known things
in black and white, of seals and walruses and bears
and caribou in ivory or rock; the close dark hives
of igloos; fish. A soapstone woman kneels,
her two white plaits escaping from her hood.

Here are the huntings and migrations,
kayaks and dog-teams and pack-sledges
carved out of stone or horn, and polished smooth
as if by ice. Here is the owl-man waiting, here's the wife
stretching her skins, the otter suckling, the two bears in rut.

The Inuit mother in her dark *aumak*
is a girl with two heads: her new-born child
grows from her shoulders. Everything she sees
her child sees too, each tiny carving cries
its uses. Every toothpick is a small harpoon.

Two seated figures hold their arms outstretched
from their muffled trunks, as if each contact hurts.
The cribbage boards are little ivory boats
with bears for figureheads, their intricate pale decks
pierced by ten dozen holes.

Hanged Man

(after the Marseilles Tarot)

For him the world is upside-down:
his head brushes a ceiling
of rotting leaves and needles, spines,
where seedlings open downwards to the sun.

Beneath his trailing foot
the great green bowls of trees
are full of wind and birdsong – and a flash
of tail. A squirrel streaks

feet uppermost. Birds swim from branch to branch.
A tree-bole swells towards a sky of earth,
the runnels of its bark
deep-fissured. Listening ears

of fungus graze his ears as he rotates.
His head is pulsing blood, his eyes
are beating with his heart; his scalp-hair lifts
and sweeps the moss, and waves, and sways.

Just to keep that one leg cocked
as if he were casual in death
is all that matters. He half-smiles.
His body pirouettes

on air and rope and rustling leaves and green
sunlight as he waits to be cut down.

Island

Twice an hour there are always people leaving
back and forth, boats meeting and crossing

for the island, always the same goodbye,
the same arrival. The same island, only older –

ferry berth displaced, the trippers changing
language, clothes and country – yet we still come back

to the same old sun, this line of graveyard hulks
at anchor on the mainland, rotting to carcasses

in saltmarsh grass, that endless spit of sand
with the amplified umbrellas. Long after dark

we all come back; the barren lump of rock
mid-channel seems to approach, recede

into nothing. Gulls ghost in and out
between one stretch of blackened water and the next,

stitching the cobbled seam we leave behind.

Return to Limenas

We've made it back. For three whole days
we dragged our own hot weight
up mountainsides – our rented bikes
our six score years, our rucksacks and injuries –
and flew back down, the wind fingering our flesh
and filling our salt-stained shirts, our eyes
crying behind their shades.

Yet from our balcony at Scala Marión
we looked clear down to the turquoise rocks.
At Pefkari the kite-men hung
lop-sided in harnesses,
grazing the surface glitter with their feet,
then winched to safety as the boat
rocked motorless. And though the sun has set
the rising parachute still floats
skirting the headland in a swirl of red.

Now we can sit and taste the cold
that rises white as smoke
over ice in our glasses; now
we can outstare the path the sun unrolls
from us to the mountain, already black
and cooling, notched with the road we took.

They

They are everywhere along the harbourfront,
the little cats, ears pricked, their legs
as delicate as sticks, the narrow feline faces
heart-shaped, rippled like sand or feathers,
big eyes flashing yellow in the dark.

They pad from place to place,
tipping their shadow-bodies from the sanded wood
of the taverna's deck onto the beach,
then wrap themselves around the plastic legs
of tables, begging to be fed.

Lean down to stroke them, and you almost drown
in purring: up here we eat fish
or chicken, calamari, fruit,
while under us the sand is steadily lapped clean,
every last crumb, as if we've never lived.

Last thing, when the restaurants are closing,
the cats still slink along
under the loungers, pour themselves from deep
shadow into shadow, the whole harbour black
except for floating stars, that sudden light

beyond the jetty as the sea
bares its white teeth. The little cats
escape to sleep our human diet off
almost unnoticed, as if replete.

Limenas

Here, in darkness, in the open square,
a boy and girl are playing
some kind of game.
Is she a cat? A little dog? She sits
up on her haunches, begging,
while he strokes her fur,
her eyes a gleam of gold,
her coat electric. She is completely his
and loyal, fierce as he is. He lies down
and she lies next to him,
their bodies curled,
identical. How is this possible?

But this is Greece
and summer night, and childhood
in a dappled darkness
where we eat ice-cream.

Birdsong

Thinking that somewhere there is still this
rich disharmony of chirp and twitter-
flutter, sparrow, thrush and finch
and blackbird, cadenced signature
of ring-dove cooing on a falling breath
to distant cock-crow, other creatures
scratching their distinctive sounds on waking –
is waking to find yourself years younger
in a place where silence grows to chatter,
adults talking softly underneath you,
moving about in rooms, performing gentle
ordinary tasks – refilling kettles,
slicing bread and turning on the gas,
cracking an egg into a crusted pan.
Then stairs become a shadow-staircase down
into a kitchen, out towards a garden
where already runner beans are twisting
scarlet-flowered upwards full of bees, and lilac
hangs its many heads and weeps, and light
is fingering the path, the fence, the rails
that hum already with the almost-
now-arriving first train of the morning.

Webs

This morning from the dark spruce
outside my door, a single filament
twists and catches light. Something has worked at this

unseen in the early morning. How did she do it? How,
in that sunlit churchyard by the Baltic where
they buried Ingmar Bergman, did a whole small crowd

of extras spool themselves right out
from head to foot of every grave? How could they float like that
across the yards of turf to find an anchorage?

They must prefer the houses of the dead
where they can string their weightless tightropes out and out
and a line might hold.

The Thought Snail

It drops on my desk like luck,
a small pale glob of something
next to my computer,
as if from a roosting bird
but half-transparent. Whitish. Wait –
a tentacle emerges, then another,
and it slides itself
towards my laptop, climbs the cave-mouth cliff
by the USB port, inches its way across
the Dolby label's green-and-silver leaf
to the distant mouse-pad,
crosses the left click
and hangs, its belly to the orange light
that means the battery's charging,
curls itself about
and travels like a spreading spill
of honey on the casing,
its soft shell
abraded on one side,
secreting this thin path
to another cliff-edge – and suspends itself
then plops
to land on hardwood like a ball of spit,
its wrinkled skin shrunk back
into the whorls of dark.
I search for it
and see it creeping out,
a single eyeball waving on its stalk –
then put the magnifying glass away
and try to write. I know it's here somewhere,
advancing inch by inch
towards a window, pale foot pressed
to a translucent comma,
resting in the giant shadow
of some other chair.

Writing in One Loft and Feeling Homesick for Another

Where there are pines there would be lavender,
a view of field with horses. In the corner
an ageing chest-of-drawers would gape its emptiness.

A bed where the desk is now, no skylight there.
Where there is ceiling sloping to the floor
would be a knee-high window with a downwards stare

over creeper, apple-orchard, bench
and animal-rescue chickens. Where there is chair
there would be chair, and banisters; this ladder would be stairs.

This lounge below would be a kitchen – room to cook and sit
and read the paper, eat together, do a crossword, drink.
The music and the scissors would be sink.

I look through trees towards the distant feet
of mountains and imagine farmyard, line of drying sheets
and pillow-slips, a garage-barn with someone else's car.

It's dark already there. The evening sun
has moved on westwards, chickens fed and up
on perches, roosting in their coop.

Somewhere a barn-owl hoots, a rabbit squeals,
a car-door slams. The sound of voices rises in the lane.
But I can hear horses breathing in their field.

Why

A telegraph-wire bounces gently in the wind
and just beyond
the roof of the house opposite
appears to move: the wire's a skipping-rope
the tiles are jumping. The way a train
eases itself smoothly from a station
making your own train move. How in a vintage boat
a tilting hammock swings
and doesn't sway an inch, the seas themselves
wrenched into wrinkles like a familiar face
that seems to be grimacing –
or have I got that wrong? How we ourselves
if we could just fly backwards fast enough
in supersonic shuttles, could make our own shadow
glide into stillness. Or how a child
runs at a down escalator and tries to climb –
why did we always do that? Or a girl shifting her weight
to tilt a see-saw at the winter sky
yet never touch the buffers. The way a rusty swing
if you work it hard enough
moves the horizon.

Again

(after the short film, Sensorium, *by animator Karen Aqua
and composer Ken Field)*

At first it is a single glowing cell
then two that meet and part; then three
red flames, budding and rippling up
through black. A lilting halo

mambos to music in a green star of shoots
then tilts to a sharpened wedge of pink
and marries it like a finger. A wisp of smoke
unlooses, swaying blue and luminous

as a bemused snake – then crankhandles out,
replaced by a pair of threads,
magenta turquoise flesh that interlocks
and swells and gives – withdraws

through swollen lips. A gold fruit rocks
in the wet crescent of the moon's mouth
and the snake uncoils, the glossy pulsing heart
has reproduced itself, the screen dividing

and dividing, each new-born square alive
to pump and dance and jiggle up down up
to split again, baroque
as a jumping quilt – and fades

to a pair of chalky smears first blue
then red-green-black and
credits. Outside, the freezing rain
has coated the trees with grey

and nothing moves
but drops like dribble sliding from a cold chin,
each twig encased in ice. *The end.*
I'll click the button, watch it through again.